Twenty to **Stitch**

Fabric Buttons

Gina Barrett

Search Press

First published in 2019

Search Press Limited
Wellwood, North Farm Road,
Tunbridge Wells, Kent TN2 3DR

Text copyright © Gina Barrett 2019

Photographs by Fiona Murray

Photography and design copyright
© Search Press Ltd. 2019

ISBN: 978-1-78221-759-6

Publishers' note
The Publishers and author can accept no
responsibility for any consequences arising from
the information, advice or instructions given in
this publication.

Readers are permitted to reproduce any
of the items in this book for their personal use,
or for the purposes of selling for charity, free of
charge and without the prior permission of the
Publishers. Any use of the items for commercial
purposes is not permitted without the prior
permission of the Publishers.

Suppliers
If you have difficulty in obtaining any of
the materials and equipment mentioned
in this book, then please visit the Search Press
website for details of suppliers:
www.searchpress.com

Visit the Twenty to Make website:
www.20toMake.com

Dedication
To my Mom and Mark.

Contents

Introduction 4

Materials, tools and techniques 6

Flower 8

Paisley 10

Boho Toggle 12

Envelope Toggle 14

Dotted Singleton 16

Kelly 18

Bow 20

Trinket 22

Rivet 24

Sunshine 26

Pod 28

Bottle-top 30

Garden 32

Cushion 34

Crown 36

Shell 38

Wrapped Up 40

'X' Marks the Spot 42

Spiral 44

Laced Up 46

Author's note 48

Introduction

Creating your own buttons is a great way to add a unique feature
to any hand-crafted project, from papercraft and journalling to
making accessories and, of course, clothing. Making fabric
buttons can be incredibly relaxing: using offcuts of fabric, each
button can be a little work of art.

My love of button-making started during my studies of early
passementerie techniques. The hand-crafted trimmings that
embellish old garments are usually overlooked by costume
historians, yet they are often the very aspect that finishes and
unifies a garment. As I have got to grips with the techniques,
I've been asked to create bespoke buttons for costumiers for
a variety of uses, from modern one-off wedding gowns and
designer coats to historical buttons for museums and films. I'm
always learning too: as my collection of original antique and
vintage *passementerie* buttons grows, so does my knowledge of
the techniques.

Button-making really can be a bit of an addiction – I love it for
so many reasons besides the historical aspect. It's a social craft
– you can work on fabric buttons while sitting with the family. My
workshops are chatty, social events as in most cases everyone is
still able to talk and work at the same time. You can take projects
to work on while travelling or sitting in a waiting room. Making
buttons is also a way to get those creative juices flowing. While
I'm working on one design I'll often have an idea for a variation, or
another design altogether.

Ultimately, it is satisfying to wear a black coat with fantastic
handcrafted buttons that replace the standard buttons supplied!

Materials, tools and techniques

For the projects in this book, I have tried to ensure that a minimum of specialist materials or tools are required.

You'll need button moulds for some of these projects – the mould is the inside of a button that gives it the shape. Choose rings that are solid (split rings are not suitable). Circle moulds can be anything round – from wooden shapes to a thin button used upside down or simply cut out from thick cardboard. Just remember that your materials, including your moulds, should be washable if you wish to wash the button. Otherwise, as when using cardboard, remove the button before washing the garment.

Note

A knowledge of basic embroidery stitches is required to embellish many of the buttons in this book.

Note

The materials listed for each project are for one button.

Your basic toolkit

For most of the buttons in this book, your basic toolkit will need to include: scissors, ruler, needles, sewing thread, stuffing (cotton wool balls work well) and a pencil or pen to mark the fabrics. A pair of compasses, circle gauges to mark out even divisions and acrylic templates for patterns can be a great help but are not essential. A small stick will come in handy to push stuffing into small spaces.

As the buttons are small, your stitches should also be small – your selection of needles should be fine, and should include chenille or milliner's needles.

Your basic toolkit for making fabric buttons.

Joining front to back

Most of the buttons in this book have a separate back to ensure that the raw edges and stitching are concealed.

Place the wrong sides together before stitching. In most instances, the front can be stitched to the back using ladder stitch (right). Felt backs are usually more easily secured using a very small whipstitch.

If you are intending to glue the button to an item such as a purse or notebook, the back can be omitted.

back

front

A diagram of ladder stitch joining the back to the front of a button.

Finishing your button

Throughout the book you will notice the phrase 'finish as required'. Any fabric button can be sewn onto a garment by stitching directly onto it. However, I recommend that whenever possible, you add a thread loop shank or stitch on a small closed jump ring for buttons that are to be used on a garment. Alternatively, use a button pin. This will help to protect your button, as the stitching can be through the loop, allowing the button to be removed more easily in the future – after all, people tend to keep pretty buttons long after the life of a garment!

Conversely, if you are using the button for a crafting project, you can finish it by adding a brooch back, a loop to make a pendant or earrings, or simply glue it into place.

Working a loop shank

With decorative thread, create a loop on the back of the button by first forming a small stitch.

1 Instead of pulling the stitch all the way through the fabric, loop a second length of thread through the stitch and hold it a little distance away (the area marked with a dot).

2 Weave the decorative thread back and forth over the two sides of the first loop until you reach the end.

3 Ensure that the weaving is tight and even. Remove the holding thread and take the end of the decorative thread back through the fabric close to the original stitches to create the loop. Secure with a knot.

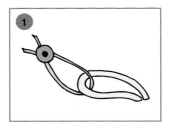
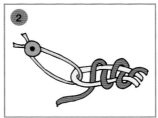
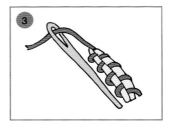

Flower

Materials:

Felt: Two flowers cut using the template below
Stranded embroidery cotton (two or three colours)
Cotton wool (for stuffing)

Tools:

Basic toolkit (see page 6)

Instructions:

1 With two strands of cotton, embroider a flower onto the right side of one piece of felt using lazy daisy stitch.

2 Again with two strands of thread, work French or colonial knots at the flower centre.

3 Cut out the two flower shapes (the embroidered flower plus one plain) – these will be the front and back of the button.

4 Place the two pieces of felt together (wrong sides facing each other) and work blanket stitch around the edges to join the two. Use two strands of thread. Work one longer stitch between each petal and keep the stitches quite close together.

5 Before the two pieces are fully stitched together, add a little bit of stuffing. Use a stick to ease stuffing into the petals. Close the gap with more blanket stitches.

6 Finish as required.

The flower template.

The finished button.

Paisley

Materials:

Felt: Two paisley shapes cut using the template below – these should be mirror-image if the felt has a wrong side.

Cotton perlé size 8 (two or three colours)

Cotton wool (for stuffing)

Tools:

Basic toolkit (see page 6)

Instructions:

1 Follow the grey lines on the template. Work one row of chain stitch on the middle line and backstitch on the other two lines. Start at the centre and work outwards.

2 Work French or colonial knots between the chain stitch and the outer line and individual stitches between the chain stitch and inner line.

3 Cut out both shapes – these will be the front and back.

4 Place the two pieces of felt together (wrong sides facing each other) and work blanket stitch around the edges to join the two. Keep the stitches quite close together.

5 Before the two pieces are fully stitched together, add a little bit of stuffing. Use a stick to ease some stuffing into the point. Close the gap with more blanket stitches.

6 Finish as required.

The paisley template.

The finished button.

Boho Toggle

Materials:

Fabric base: One 40 x 30mm (1½ x 1¼in) strip

Decorative fabric (choose a fabric that frays easily):
  One 25 x 40mm (1 x 1½in) strip
  One 15 x 40mm (½ x 1½in) strip

Felt: One 25 x 15mm (1 x ½in) strip

Cotton perlé size 8

Tools:

Basic toolkit (see page 6)

Iron

The finished button.

Instructions:

1 Place the felt piece on the wrong side of the base fabric. Fold the two short sides in, over the felt, and tack into place. Press.

2 Roll the rectangle along the longest length, then stitch along the edge to hold.

3 Place the small decorative strip on top of the larger strip. Fold one short end in towards the wrong side and press. Starting with the raw edge, wrap this double strip around the base toggle, then ladder stitch the folded edge.

4 Using perlé thread, work four rows of small running stitches around the central area of the toggle. Take the stitches through to catch the fabric of the base toggle.

5 When the stitching is complete, use the needle to pull out the edge threads of both decorative fabrics at either side to create a frayed edge.

6 Finish as required.

Note

Stitch only the centre of the decorative fabric to ensure that the edges can be frayed.

Envelope Toggle

Materials:

Decorative fabric: One 35 x 50mm (1½ x 2in) strip

Felt: One 20 x 15mm (¾ x ½in) strip

Cotton perlé size 8

Tools:

Basic toolkit (see page 6)

Iron

Instructions:

The finished button.

1 Fold each long end of the fabric 5mm (¼in) into the wrong side and press.

2 Fold one short end 5mm (¼in) into the wrong side and press, then fold in the corners of this end to create a point. Press again and secure with a small stitch through the folded section only.

3 Place the felt above the point and tack to the turned-in edge. Do not stitch through to the right side.

4 Using the cotton perlé, work a small running stitch along the edges and part of the point. There is no need to stitch the actual point. A light press from the wrong side will meld these stitches.

5 Starting from the raw edge, fold and add a few holding stitches. Roll the strip, adding a few holding stitches without going through to the right side. When the strip is fully rolled, use the cotton perlé to work a few stitches to hold down the point.

6 Finish as required.

Dotted Singleton

Materials:

Fabric: One circle cut using the green template (see below)
One circle cut using the blue template (see below)

Felt: One circle cut using the black template (see below)

19mm (¾in) brass ring

Variegated stranded embroidery cotton

Tools:

Basic toolkit (see page 6)

Circle templates. Note that some of these coloured circles are used as templates later in the book.

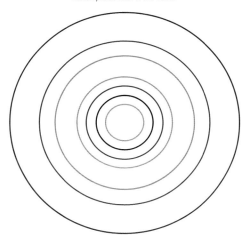

The finished buttons.

Instructions:

1 Thread a sharp needle with sewing thread and knot the end. Work a small backstitch approximately 5mm (¼in) in from the edge of the largest circle. Now work small running stitches all of the way around.

2 Gather the thread to begin to form a pouch shape, with the right side facing out.

3 Insert the ring and pull in the stitches to tighten them around the ring. Work a small backstitch to hold the gathers.

4 Work long stitches from top to bottom across the back of the button in a spiral. Each stitch should catch just a small amount of the fabric, and pull in towards the centre. This will tighten the fabric across the face of the button.

5 Using two strands of embroidery cotton, work French or colonial knots at random on a portion of the button. Each should be worked up through the fabric in the section inside of the ring.

6 Cover the piece of felt with the smaller circle using the above method to form the back. Take care to keep the felt flat. Tack the edge of the fabric to the felt if required.

7 Join the front to the back and finish as required.

Tip

Use seed beads or small individual stitches instead of knots for a different look.

The singleton method

Steps 1 to 4 are used to cover button moulds, rings and backings throughout the book. Simply insert the relevant piece or stuffing at step 3. The spiral stitches will need to be less tight when covering a soft item such as felt to maintain the shape. These steps will be referred to hereafter as **the singleton method.**

Kelly

Materials:

Fabric: One 15 x 250mm (½ x 9¾in) bias strip
   One circle cut using the green template (see page 16)

Felt: One circle cut using the red template (see page 16)

20mm (¾in) plastic ring

Cotton wool (for stuffing)

Tools:

Basic toolkit (see page 6)

PVA glue

Instructions:

1 Fold the bias strip in half lengthwise.

2 Glue one end to the plastic ring and wrap the ring with the fabric – each wrap should be placed so that the fold covers the raw edge of the previous wrap. Stretch the bias strip as you wrap.

3 When you have a few wraps left, fold both ends of the bias strip in towards the centre of the strip. This is a little difficult at first, but each wrap will get easier. Continue to wrap and the last wrap should then have both raw edges folded in.

4 Stitch the end of the strip to the fabric at the back of the ring to hold it. Do not trim off the excess yet.

5 Use the singleton method (see page 16) to create a half ball shape using the circle of fabric and some stuffing. Before tightening, ensure that the shape will fit into the centre of the ring and adjust the stuffing if required.

6 Push the half ball up through the centre of the ring. Secure in place by stitching the back of the half ball and catching the bias fabric at the edge. The back of the button should be flat.

7 Any excess from the bias strip can also be stitched to the back of the half ball before being trimmed. This will help to ensure that it is well secured.

8 Stitch the felt to the back of the button, using small stitches and trimming it if required.

9 Finish as required.

The finished button.

Bow

Materials:

Fabric: One circle cut using the green template (see page 16) for the centre
One circle cut using the blue template (see page 16) for the back
One bias strip 15 x 210mm (½ x 8¼in) for the surround
One straight strip 20 x 70mm (¾ x 2¾in) for the bow (lightweight silk or similar is best)

Felt: Three circles cut using the black template (see page 16)

20mm (¾in) plastic ring

Stranded embroidery cotton (optional)

Tools:

Basic toolkit (see page 6)

PVA glue

Instructions:

1 Fold the bias strip in half lengthwise and cover the ring in the same way as the *Kelly* button (see pages 18–19).

2 Cover two of the felt pieces with the large circle of fabric using the singleton method (see page 16).

3 Fold each long raw edge of the straight cut strip in towards the centre. Gather at the centre of the strip to form a bow shape.

4 Place the bow centrally on the shape created in step 2, stitching it in place at the centre. If you wish, use one or two strands of embroidery thread at the centre to emphasize this part.

5 Wrap the two ends of the strip around the shape, twisting at the back a little to form a more natural shape. Take care not to expose the raw edges on the front. Stitch the strips to secure at the back of the shape, and trim the excess.

6 Bring the shape up through the centre of the ring and stitch the ring and shape together at the back. Stitch the excess from step 1 onto the pad for a clean finish.

7 Cover the remaining piece of felt with the smaller circle using the singleton method to form the back. Take care to keep the felt flat. Tack the edge of the fabric to the felt if required.

8 Join front to back (see page 7) and finish as required.

The finished button.

Trinket

Materials:

Fabric: Two circles cut using the blue template (see page 16)

Felt: One circle cut using the grey template (see page 16)

13mm (½in) brass ring

Stranded embroidery cotton

11/0 seed beads

Tools:

Basic toolkit (see page 6)

Beading needle

The finished button.

Instructions:

1 Cover the ring with one circle of fabric using the singleton method (see page 16).

2 Using two strands of embroidery cotton, work small backstitches in a circle just inside the ring.

3 Using one strand of embroidery cotton and a beading needle, add the beads to the edge of the ring in the following way: work blanket stitches from the back along the edge of the ring. Before taking the thread back into the fabric at each stitch, add a bead, then proceed with the blanket stitch.

4 When all of the beads have been added, take the thread through all of them once or twice in a circle, before securing the thread at the reverse.

5 Cover the piece of felt with the remaining circle using the singleton method to form the back. Take care to keep the felt flat. Tack the edge of the fabric to the felt if required.

6 Join front to back (see page 7) and finish as required.

Rivet

Materials:

Fabric: One circle cut using the green template (see page 16)
   One circle cut using the blue template (see page 16)
   One bias strip 15 x 110mm ($\frac{1}{2}$ x 4$\frac{1}{4}$in)

Pelmet interfacing: One circle cut using the black template (see page 16)

13mm ($\frac{1}{2}$in) brass ring

19mm ($\frac{3}{4}$in) brass ring

Metallic effect embroidery thread

Tools:

Basic toolkit (see page 6)

Clear-drying glue

Circle gauge to mark divisions
   (optional)

The finished button.

Instructions:

1 Fold the bias strip in half lengthwise and cover the small ring in the same way as for the *Kelly* button (see pages 18–19).

2 Cover the large ring with the large circle of fabric using the singleton method (see page 16).

3 Place the small ring on top of the front of the large ring and secure in place with very small stitches. These should be worked catching the outer edge of the small ring and going through the fabric on the large ring.

4 Mark five divisions on the edge of the button. Using a metallic thread, work straight stitches over the small ring and the edge of the large ring. Work as many stitches as required to create a band at each division. These stitches are not only decorative, but will also help to ensure that the small ring is secure.

5 Cover the interfacing with the small circle of fabric using the singleton method to form the back.

6 Join front to back (see page 7) and finish as required.

Sunshine

Materials:

Fabric: One circle cut using the pink template (see page 16)
  One circle cut using the green template (see page 16)

Felt: One circle cut using the black template (see page 16)

20mm (¾in) plastic ring

Stranded embroidery cotton (two colours)

8/0 seed beads

Sewing thread (optional)

Tools:

Basic toolkit (see page 6)

Beading needle

Circle gauge to mark divisions
  (optional)

Instructions:

1 Cover the ring with the large circle using the singleton method (see page 16).

2 Mark twelve divisions around the edge. With the first colour, use three strands of embroidery cotton to work a stitch around the ring at each mark.

3 With the second colour, thread the needle with six strands of embroidery cotton. Bring the thread up at the centre of the button. Take the thread under one stitch created in the first step. This stitch now becomes number one. Take the thread down to number seven – counting clockwise – and then under this stitch. The thread now needs to go up to stitch two and under it, then down to stitch eight and under it. Continue in this way, working in a clockwise direction until all stitches have a thread loop through them. Take the thread back down to the back at the centre of the button.

4 Using sewing thread or one strand of embroidery cotton, stitch five beads at the centre of the button. Ensure that the beads are well secured.

5 Cover the piece of felt with the small circle using the singleton method to form the back. Take care to keep the felt flat. Tack the edge of the fabric to the felt if required.

6 Join front to back (see page 7) and finish as required.

The finished button.

Pod

Materials:

Fabric: One circle cut using the pink template (see page 16)
 Two circles cut using the green template (see page 16)

Felt: One circle cut using the blue template (see page 16)

20mm (¾in) circle button mould

Seed beads to match fabric

Tools:

Basic toolkit (see page 6)

Beading needle

Instructions:

1 Turn in the edge of one of the smaller fabric circles a little and work a running stitch over this. Gather this in quite tightly, but not fully closed, to make the pod shape. Ensure that the right side is facing out.

2 Stitch the pod onto the large circle of fabric. The pod should be placed off centre. Check its placement before stitching: the pod should not go over the edge of the mould.

3 Using a beading needle, stitch seed beads into the opening of the pod.

4 Cover the button mould with the large circle of fabric using the singleton method (see page 16). However, before placing the button mould into the fabric, put the piece of felt inside. Then place the mould on the felt, and continue to tighten the cover. This will soften the top and edges of the button slightly and give cushioning for the beads. Remember to check the placement of the pod before tightening the covering.

5 Fold in the raw edge of the remaining fabric circle and stitch this to the back of the button.

6 Finish as required.

The finished button.

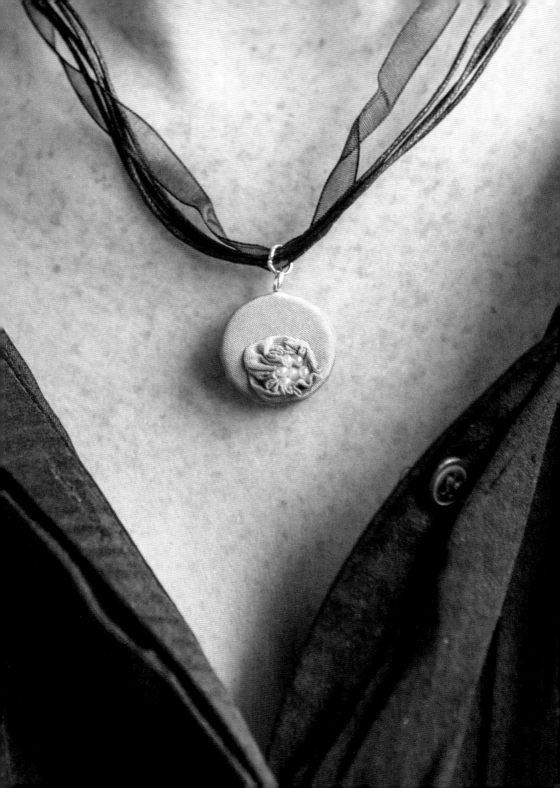

Bottle-top

Materials:

A small bottle top (from a water bottle or smaller)

Fabric: The size will depend on the size of the bottle top. Follow the instructions to make the pattern first. It is a good idea to have scrap fabric for your first pattern, to test it.

Cotton wool (for stuffing)

Tools:

Basic toolkit (see page 6)

PVA glue

Ruler

Pair of compasses

Instructions:

1 Unroll a ball of cotton wool and wrap it around the side of the bottle top and tuck over the edge to the inside. Do not fill the top – the cotton wool is to soften the edge only. It should not be too thick. Do not have any cotton wool on the flat part of the bottle top – this will be the base of the button.

2 Measure the height of the side and the width of the base, taking into account the cotton wool.

3 Add together the measurement of the base and 3 x the sides. If the bottle top has very high sides, you may need to calculate 4 x the sides. This is the size of circle A.

4 Add together the measurement of the base and one side. This is the size for circle B.

5 Cut one circle A. Cover the wrapped bottle top using the singleton method (see page 16) with the flat part of the bottle top inside against the fabric. Push the gathered edge into the bottle top, adding a little bit of PVA glue to help the fabric stay along the inside edge of the top.

6 Cut one circle B. Stitch along the edge and gather up, then stuff to create a ball. Check that it fits inside the bottle top, and adjust the stuffing if required. Stitch together the raw edges.

7 Add a small amount of glue to the inside of the bottle top and place the ball inside with the stitched side facing down. Press in well.

8 Use a ladder stitch to sew the centre to the sides.

9 Finish as required.

The finished buttons.

Garden

Materials:

Fabric: One bias strip 25 x 50mm (1 x 2in) – lightweight silk or similar is best

Felt: One circle cut using the grey template (see page 16)

Cotton wool (for stuffing)

Stranded embroidery cotton (at least two colours)

Tools:

Basic toolkit (see page 6)

The finished button.

Instructions:

1 Start with a backstitch and work a running stitch along one long side of the fabric strip. Gather up the side tightly and work a stitch or two to hold the gathers.

2 Ensure that the right sides are together, and stitch together the two short sides. Fasten off the thread.

3 Turn out to the right side. Stuff the shape, but not too firmly.

4 Gather the base to close it and flatten the shape a little to get a flat base before tightening it completely.

5 Use one or two strands of embroidery cotton to embroider random flowers, grass, leaves and dots. Place a small flower in lazy daisy stitch at the top to disguise the gathered area.

6 Stitch the felt to the back of the button, using small stitches and trimming it if required.

7 Finish as required.

Cushion

Materials:

Fabric: One circle cut using the pink template (see page 16)
One circle cut using the green template (see page 16)

Felt: One circle cut using the red template (see page 16)

Wadding (see note below): Two circles cut using the red template (see page 16)

Pelmet interfacing: One circle cut using the red template (see page 16)
One square cut using the green template (see below, right)

Cotton perlé size 8

Tools:

Basic toolkit (see page 6)

Instructions:

1 Using the large fabric circle, cover the two pieces of wadding and one piece of felt using the singleton method (see page 16). Ensure that the wadding is placed inside first, and then the felt. Tighten to secure, but not too much. Over-tightening will diminish the effect of the wadding.

2 Place the small square at the centre of the button face. This will act as a guide for the central stitches. Using sewing thread, make a tight stitch at each side of the square. Do not sew through the square. Pull the stitches in to create a cushioned effect. Remove the square.

3 Over-stitch these stitches twice with cotton perlé. You will have a neater finish by making two single stitches as opposed to making one stitch with double thread.

4 Work two long stitches out from each diagonal, taking the thread to the reverse of the button each time to secure it. These stitches should be a little tight, enough to create a small depression, but not as deep as those at the centre.

5 Cover the interfacing with the smaller piece of fabric using the singleton method to form the back.

6 Join front to back (see page 7) and finish as required.

Note

The wadding will be difficult to mark. Instead, cut the interfacing first, and use this as a template to cut around.

The finished button.

Square templates. Note that some of these coloured squares are used as templates later in the book.

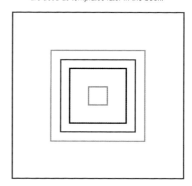

Crown

Materials:

Fabric: One circle cut using the green template (see page 16)
One circle cut using the blue template (see page 16)

Felt: One circle cut using the black circle template (see page 16)

Pelmet interfacing: One circle cut using the black template (see page 16)

Wadding (see note below): Two circles cut using the black template (see page 16)

Cotton perlé size 8

6/0 bead

Sewing thread

Tools:

Basic toolkit (see page 6)

Circle gauge to mark divisions (optional)

Long milliner's needle

Awl to make a hole (optional)

Instructions:

1 Poke a small hole in the centre of the interfacing.

2 Using the largest fabric circle, cover the two pieces of wadding and one piece of interfacing using the singleton method (see page 16). Ensure that the wadding is placed inside first, then the interfacing. Tighten to secure, but not too much. Over-tightening will diminish the effect of the wadding.

3 With sewing thread, come up through the hole in the interfacing to the face of the button, and then back down again to the back, pulling the stitch to create a small dimple at the centre.

4 Mark six divisions and work a long bullion stitch (see below) over the face of the button at each mark. You will need about seventeen wraps for each bullion.

5 Add a bead at the centre.

6 Cover the piece of felt with the smaller circle using the singleton method to form the back. Take care to keep the felt flat. Tack the edge of the fabric to the felt if required.

7 Join front to back (see page 7) and finish as required.

Note

The wadding will be difficult to mark. Instead, cut the interfacing first, and use this as a template to cut around.

The long bullion

1 Bring the needle up through the centre

2 Take it around the button and up through the centre again but do not pull it all the way through.

3 Wrap the thread that is at the centre around the needle as many times as required.

4 Draw the needle and thread through, while holding the wraps, then take the needle around the button and up through the centre (becoming step 1 again) and tighten.

The finished button.

Shell

Materials:

Fabric: Two shells cut using template B below

Felt: Two shells cut using template A below

Pelmet interfacing: One shell cut using template A below

Stranded embroidery cotton

6/0 bead

Tools:

Basic toolkit (see page 6)

Instructions:

1 Mark the stitching lines of template B onto one of the fabric pieces.

2 Cover the two pieces of felt with the marked fabric piece. The easiest way to do this is to fold over the fabric edges and to stitch these onto the felt. Ensure that the marked lines face out. The wavy edge does not need to be exact; the felt will help to create the shape.

3 Using one strand of the embroidery cotton, work fine running stitches over the marked lines. Work these through the fabric only – do not go through the felt filling, except to move along to the next row.

4 Secure a bead to the front of the stitched piece.

5 Cover the piece of interfacing with the remaining fabric piece using the singleton method (see page 16) to form the back. You will need to tighten the fabric carefully to ensure that the shell shape is maintained.

6 Join front to back (see page 7) and finish as required.

The finished button.

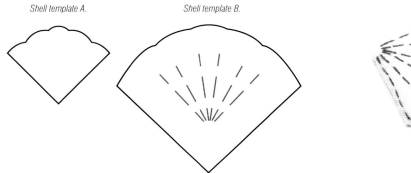

Shell template A.

Shell template B.

Wrapped Up

Materials:

Fabric: Two squares cut using the pink template (see page 34)

Pelmet interfacing: One square cut using the red template (see page 34)

Cotton perlé size 8 (two colours)

Tools:

Basic toolkit (see page 6)

Iron

Instructions:

1 Fold one piece of fabric diagonally – matching two corners – and finger-press at the centre, then unfold. Now, fold diagonally, matching the other corners, and finger-press at the centre, then unfold. The place where the finger-pressed lines meet is the centre of the square. Mark this on the wrong side.

2 With the right side facing down, fold the corners in to the centre mark. Press.

3 Repeat, folding each new corner in to the centre and place a small stitch to hold. Do not press these folds.

4 Secure a length of cotton perlé to the smooth side (the back) of the fabric and wrap around the centre of the shape four times. Secure again at the back and then wrap in the opposite direction four times to form a cross.

5 With the second colour of cotton perlé, work three crossed stitches at the centre of the wrapped cross to hold it in securely, and then work a single stitch on each fold to ensure that they remain in place.

6 Cover the interfacing with the remaining square using the singleton method (see page 16) to form the back. You will need to tighten the fabric carefully to ensure that the square shape is maintained.

7 Join front to back (see page 7) and finish as required.

The finished button.

'X' Marks the Spot

Materials:

Fabric: Two squares cut using the blue template (see page 34)

Felt: Two squares cut using the black template (see page 34)

Pelmet interfacing: One square cut using the black template (see page 34)

Cotton perlé size 8

Tools:

Basic toolkit (see page 6)

Iron

Instructions:

1 Cover the two pieces of felt with one square of fabric using the singleton method (see page 16). You may need to tack the fabric to the felt to ensure that the square shape is maintained.

2 Cover the interfacing with the remaining square in the same way, tightening carefully to ensure that the square shape is maintained.

3 Secure a length of the cotton perlé to the back of the felt padded square. Wrap from corner to corner, secure with a stitch at the back, then repeat for the other corner side to form a cross. Come up from the back and add one small stitch at the centre to hold the cross straight. Take the thread down to the back.

4 Bring up the thread alongside one of the lines about 2mm (¾in) from the corner. Take the thread in a straight line to the next diagonal, and go down to the back. Come back up and repeat on all four sides to create a square.

5 Come up again right below the first stitch. Take the thread around the corner threads – including the diagonal – then move along to the next corner. Work around this to the next corner and repeat. Continue in this way, each time wrapping around and under the previous threads until you reach the centre. Do not go through the fabric. At the centre, take the thread through to the back and fasten off.

6 Join front to back (see page 7) and finish as required.

The finished button.

Spiral

Materials:

Fabric: One bias strip 190 x 15mm (7½ x ½in)
   One circle cut using the blue template (see page 16)
Pelmet interfacing: One circle cut using the black template (see page 16)
190mm (7½in) satin cord
6/0 seed beads

Tools:

Basic toolkit (see page 6)

Instructions:

1 Fold the bias strip around the cord to encase it. Tack along the cord to hold the fabric in place.

2 Start from one end and coil the covered cord, tucking the end to the back. As you roll, stitch to hold the spiral in place. Keep your stitches as close to the cord as possible and take care to ensure that the raw edge remains at the bottom. The spiral should finish at about 20mm (¾in).

3 Trim away any excess fabric so that the button is not too deep – take care not to cut into your stitches. Tuck the end of the spiral to the back and stitch to secure.

4 Stitch beads in a line from the centre out to the end of the spiral. This will help to disguise the uneven edge caused by the cord finishing. Ensure that the beads are well secured.

5 Use the circle to cover the interfacing using the singleton method (see page 16) to form the back.

6 Join front to back (see page 7) and finish as required.

The finished button.

Laced Up

Materials:

Fabric: One circle cut using the purple template (see page 16)
One circle cut using the green template (see page 16)

Felt: One circle cut using the red template (see page 16)
One circle cut using the blue template (see page 16)

25mm (1in) circle button mould

Cotton perlé size 8

Tools:

Basic toolkit (see page 6)

Iron

Instructions:

1 Fold the large circle in half and finger-press to mark the centre. Unfold.

2 Fold one side over about 5mm (¼in) from the centre pressed line. At the centre, fold the side back out to form a pleat. Repeat with the other side, then press.

3 Carefully cover the mould and matching felt circle with the pleated fabric using the singleton method (see page 16). The felt should be against the fabric to soften the face of the button. As the shape is somewhat oval due to the pleat, take care when tightening. The pleat will open slightly, which is what is required, but do not let it fully open.

4 Using cotton perlé, work stitches back and forth across the slightly opened pleat to hold it securely and pull it in a little.

5 Cover the small piece of felt with the small circle using the singleton method to form the back. Take care to keep the felt flat. Tack the edge of the fabric to the felt if required.

6 Join front to back (see page 7) and finish as required.

The finished button.

Author's note
Button moulds, rings, circle gauges
and button templates are available
from Gina-B Silkworks:
www.ginabsilkworks.co.uk